ONLY YOU KNOW . . .

MARGARITË CAMAJ

authorHOUSE®

AuthorHouse™
1663 Liberty Drive
Bloomington, IN 47403
www.authorhouse.com
Phone: 1 (800) 839-8640

Published by AuthorHouse   05/25/2016

ISBN: 978-1-5246-1087-6 (sc)
ISBN: 978-1-5246-1085-2 (hc)
ISBN: 978-1-5246-1086-9 (e)

Library of Congress Control Number: 2016908450

Print information available on the last page.

Any people depicted in stock imagery provided by Thinkstock are models, and such images are being used for illustrative purposes only. Certain stock imagery © Thinkstock.

This book is printed on acid-free paper.

Because of the dynamic nature of the Internet, any web addresses or links contained in this book may have changed since publication and may no longer be valid. The views expressed in this work are solely those of the author and do not necessarily reflect the views of the publisher, and the publisher hereby disclaims any responsibility for them.

To: God

Thank you for everything, especially for opening my eyes and not letting me walk through life blindly. Thank you for allowing me to see things that some may not have the courage to notice or speak out about. I want to thank you for giving me a gift since I was a little girl even though sometimes it has been extremely hard to carry. Thank you for the environment that you have placed me in and thank you for the people that you have placed in my life—every single one of them. Thank you for the pain and thank you for the happiness. I hold them equally close to me. Every single situation has been a blessing, either in clear sight or in disguise. I believe that I was given this gift so that I can stay in touch with not only myself, but also every single thing and person around me. It keeps me aware and allows me to understand certain things that some may not. Though some may never understand, I know that you understanding has always been and will always be enough. If I am being honest with myself, I am confident enough to say that I have learned enough to know that in the end,

...Only You Know.

This is dedicated to every single person who feels a little lost and unsure of where life has taken them or where their path is leading them to. I hope you know that the Higher Power will always be there to guide you even when you doubt him. This goes out to anyone who feels like they are constantly reaching out for something external to heal. I just want you to know that your greatness lies within and once you align all the pieces that lie within, the universe will align all that lives outside. We are, sometimes, taught to not speak out on what we believe in because others don't believe the same. We are sometimes taught to conform to society because it is all we know. We are sometimes forced to forget about what we hold inside of us because we are so busy dealing with our day to day lives. We must stop and pay attention to the signs. Only then will everything become a little clearer. Only then will it start to make sense and connect.

This goes out to everyone who is struggling to find a place in this world. This goes out to every single human who is struggling to remain alive. Your purpose is far greater than you think right now. You being alive will save, not only you, but others too. And when the days and nights seem long and happiness is not within your search, search for the strength in your soul because I promise that it lives within you. Just hold on and you will see.

Dear Liridona Ceka,

I am beyond proud of your strength. For every dark day and night, we all have a light that is within us. And, when strength can't be found, we have angels that will bring it to us in ways that we may not understand at the moment.

Rest in Peace Almir Ceka
…You are now immortal.

...Everything connects.

I feel like time could do two things. It could either bring us closer together or it could tear us apart. Sometimes, it did both. But, I found it almost unbelievable that someone wouldn't leave my side even when I did—many times. It was like you were always there. You never left—even when I did.

Dear God,

11:03AM

3-3-2016

They asked me why I was indecisive. I asked them how could I not be? I am careful with the smallest decisions in my life—down to how I drink my tea and where I choose to sit and enjoy it. I have learned that the smallest decisions have such a great impact on my life. Every single thing is connected. Every single thing I choose affects the way my next few seconds will be. And, every single second of my life has always had purpose. I live in a world, but I also have my own. I have learned that my world is created by my choices and my choices are what brought me here. Destiny and fate play a great role, but I like to believe that I do too.

9:37PM
3-3-2016

Your existence is proof that the universe doesn't give up on you. I believe that even when you leave, your soul remains. I have always found this to be a beautiful mystery. The human is only capable of knowing so much—but believing and feeling? Now, that is a completely different experience. The heart has always, always been more powerful than the mind.

9:15AM

3-4-2016

My hands have broken, over and over again, reaching out for something that was never there. You knew all along that you were giving me something greater. Thank you.

11:52PM

3-4-2016

Thank you for teaching me that being alone is beautiful.
Thank you for teaching me that my heart is my home before
I allow strangers to enter inside and make a mess of it. You
taught me to learn every part of my heart so I not only
know how to use it to take care of myself, but others too.

1:25PM

3-5-2016

Even when it appears that they do not have a heart, help me be selfless to the point where I think that I could give them mine. Help me help them learn how to follow their hearts whenever they are in doubt. If my words do not help them, give me your power so that I can lead by example.

12:07AM
3-6-16

I took hate and created it into illusions of love. I hope I always have the power to believe in change that much. I hope that I can take my thoughts and turn them into actions, but I also pray that I won't create things that don't exist.

7:21AM
3-6-16

I have realized that not everyone has the same strength—
meaning some can pick up their broken pieces faster than
others. However, your biggest self-destruction will be if, after a
while, you fail to change feeling that you are being victimized
into realizing there are some things that can be changed
through your own power. Life happens and it can hurt so much
that you think it will kill you, but there are certain things that
you can fix yourself. Constantly blaming what is external and
pointing fingers instead of focusing on the internal will damage
you in the long run. I know because I have been there, too.

8:23AM

3-6-16

I have met laughter on even the darkest of days. So, when they ask me to explain hope—that is exactly what I will tell them. If it is possible to find moments that can make you laugh, then that is enough to keep going. It is enough power to push you to another day. I hope that I always fight for happiness and never give up. It is attainable even when your hands feel as if they can never reach it.

10:35PM

3-6-16

There are times when I feel like I don't live in this world, but instead, I fully believe that I live only in my mind. Truthfully, both places give me something different. I have found that both give me something to believe in. Both give me the strength to keep going. Help me find a balance.

6:02AM

3-7-16

I know now that it would harm me to search for meaning in everything with my eyes, but to fail to find what lies inside. In order to try to understand what lives outside of me, I must take the time to learn all of my parts. Look inside.

7:01PM

3-7-16

Gravitate me towards those who know to love every single thing in its most natural state of being before any addition because I know that anything that is added on to my being is not as raw or real. I want them to love me in the most pure way. I want them to love me just like the way you love me—to my core.

7:07AM
3-8-16

We are constantly looking for light in the darkness instead of falling in love with its beauty. We, as humans, always try to look for an alternative instead of finding the beauty in what is. We have trouble finding beauty in things as they are. We have trouble accepting things that are created without adding any additions. Allow my heart to appreciate your creation more.

1:06AM

3-9-16

Sometimes I want to talk to you because I am not sure if many in this society understand me. I am not saying that I am always right. That would be the farthest thing from the truth. I just want to know why I view love the way I do. I want to know if anyone else shares the same view. I have seen so many that are so desperate to find someone to love that they will run to anyone and anything that "loves" them. I would rather wait for real love. To me, waiting for real love overpowers living with illusions of love—forever.

7:39AM

3-9-16

When I feel so cold that I can't feel my own heartbeat, I hope I have enough trust inside of me to believe that there is someone praying that I will be able to feel once again.

11:34PM

3-9-16

If it is mine, let it be. But, if it isn't for me, then give it to someone else and bless them. Just guide me to what is for me—whatever it may be.

2:21PM

3-10-16

We live in a world where people will try to destroy the person who helped build them up, failing to realize that they are destroying the foundation, which in the long run will destroy them. Some people become so blinded to their own demise that they won't even see it. So, they fill their hearts with spite. In turn, they will do anything that might potentially destroy who you are. But, you see, when you have a strong character and soul, no one will be able to move you—let alone change you. Your silence has power. So much, that it protects who you are with no words needed. We live in a world where people create these false illusions to try to tear down what is real. This is the challenge: through all of this, keep your heart pure, keep who you are pure, and stay so focused that no one can move you—unless for the better.

10:49PM

3-10-16

I think that I have figured it out. It all comes down to this: who can't you see the rest of your life without? I will know it is real love when the thought of your absence shakes my soul and breaks all the cells of my body. I have been praying to you so that I can figure it out. You have helped me.

4:15AM

3-11-16

I noticed the ones that elevated their souls. Naturally, I noticed him. That was his secret, you know. For him, it was always about substance. He knew that he had to search deep in order to find it. It was not something that lived on the surface. He knew that it was something that only made its presence to eyes that pierced through skin and made their way to the soul. That was exactly how he found her. Her soul sparked a kind of beauty that left those who searched for substance in awe. It transformed to the physical. We are not only humans who bleed, are we? We were always more than that.

11:59PM

3-11-16

They are confused. Not everything is temporary.
There is something about love—real love—that is
immortal. Not even death can kill it. Permanence
lives in love. Just like you live in me.

2:01 AM

3-12-16

I started putting everything together and that is when I realized that the universe was not as much of a mystery as I had once thought. You see, when I went through life blindly, I did not get the answers that I wanted. But, now that I am observant, I see things that most don't because they do not search deeper. This was a blessing that I wasn't willing to ever take for granted, or give up.

3:00AM

3-12-16

I will give—even when it feels like they are taking my last breath. I will give—even when it feels like they are taking the last bits of my heart. I am stronger than they are. I am capable and that in itself is a gift because some haven't been able to reach that level of the self yet. Some aren't able to give anything—let alone their all. Don't let them kill my gift.

2:37PM

3-12-16

There are times when I see truth where others
don't. You have shown me that it is possible to have
faith and love you even when others won't.

3:05AM

3-13-16

You have shown me that life becomes a beautiful thing once you start to find the gifts hidden in all the pain. Now, I welcome it all with open arms, as if I am positive that it will teach me something huge—and at times, much bigger than even happiness could.

10:21AM

3-13-16

You usually find the most important things when you don't look for them. You just have to pay attention. I now know that my biggest mistake was that I blamed timing instead of placing the responsibility on myself. Now, I know what to do as I move ahead.

1:05AM
3-14-16

I just want to prove to them that certain things exist—like unconditional love. I want to bring it to life just so they can all witness it and so that someone else can help me fight for it, too.

9:18AM

3-14-16

I have noticed that some will treat you like you are a
mystery in desperate need of being solved and once you
are solved, they will no longer be around. I have learned to
be careful of people who treat some like things instead of
humans. But, this shouldn't make me cold because there
are others who exist that know you can't figure a soul out.
They know that a soul just exists without form. It doesn't
have a formula that the human can just figure out.

1:10AM

3-15-16

I find it most beautiful when I look directly at my scars
and start to put the pieces together and decide to heal them
by loving again. Allow my heart to be open, always.

10:01AM

3-15-16

Some people think they are free, but they are really not. Think of all that controls you. If you can't do exactly what your heart wants right now, you are not free. If you can't do what you fear most, you are not free. If you can't run towards your passion, that means you are not free. If you can't look at yourself in the mirror and know a great part of who you are, you are not free. The more that I ran away from you, the more I realized that I was not free. I have been here, but that is only existing. I find that the more that I am running towards you, the more I find myself coming alive.

1:45AM

3-16-16

Do you ever fear happiness? I do. I don't know if I trust
myself with happiness. At times, I feel as if I'll break it. Maybe
that is the problem. Other times, I feel like it is an illusion.
Help me learn to have faith even if happiness escapes me.

7:48AM

3-16-16

It is a struggle between you and I. I feel like it has always been. I doubt you every second because we fight for what is best for me every second of the day. I guess these words are just me talking to you. I'm just trying to pray.

3:15AM

3-17-16

No amount of pain could ever desensitize me. I am a human that is too full of emotions and I know that you have a bigger plan for me than I have for myself. Although I know that I play a big role, I know that it is all in your hands. I know that your plan is too calculated for me to even try to understand.

9:47AM

3-17-16

They fear solitude so much that they will settle for a love created from the mind, not the heart. I hope that my love will always flow from my heart first, without control. I am aware that they must all align, but my heart needs to feel first.

11:05PM

3-17-16

The pain has turned beautiful. On my darkest nights, I hope that I know that I just have to get through it. The seconds might feel damaging, but I need to remember to keep going. And, on the days and nights that I am most broken, I hope that I am at least a broken person whose smile can heal some.

11:31AM

3-18-16

If I ever were to forget what love is, use signs to
remind me. Show me how to open my eyes when
I have lost the ability to. Show me the way.

12:45AM

3-19-16

On the nights where I will go without sleep, I hope you show me that time is not my enemy. Comfort me in my dreams.

10:40AM

3-19-16

I woke up in peace today even though there are nights when I am completely shaken. Remind me to have hope that everything will always be okay even if my mind cannot imagine it.

12:33AM

3-20-16

Help me free my heart of what shouldn't be there. Replace it with whatever it is you think is best even if I think it isn't.

8:11AM

3-20-16

It feels like things change every day except for two things: my love and the pain. Ironic because, at times, they come hand in hand. The way I love heals everyone, but it has the potential to kill me. Then I start to think that maybe the only way to heal myself is to stop loving and to stop using my heart, but I know that I was not made to do that. I know that way of living is selfish. Whenever I feel like this, remind me that I am selfless.

2:41AM

3-21-16

I have been talking to you more lately because they are trying to make me conform. They want me to change, not grow. Save the real me.

11:35AM

3-21-16

I wonder what is going on in their minds. Sometimes, I wonder if they have an idea about all of the thoughts that go on in mine. Do they talk to you like I do? Do they believe in you? Do they think that the universe conspires so that everything can eventually connect? Help me understand them more than they understand me.

1:21AM

3-22-16

Help me take care of my soul. Keep my soul raw.
Don't let illusions pollute it. Take anything that is not
real out of it and remove it from me completely.

9:40AM
3-22-16

I have moments when it gets so dark that I
can't see. In the moments when I close my eyes
and look inward, help me find light.

7:43PM

3-22-16

Thank you for teaching me unconditional love, forgiveness, and loyalty. I have left you many times and you have still protected me, silently. You still stayed even when I didn't.

3:33PM

3-23-16

There will be moments when I won't love
myself. I will feel unworthy. These will be the
times I will need you to love me most.

3:13AM

3-24-16

When I feel like I am not good enough, fill me with trust that I am. Take away the thoughts that poison my mind and heart.

9:01AM

3-24-16

If ever I feel like I have lost hope, help me think of all the
times you have restored it when I thought I had nothing left.

2:41AM

3-25-16

I am trying to embrace my flaws, but sometimes
I feel like I am too broken and I can't be fixed.
Remind me that I am only human.

10:09AM
3-25-16

I have found gifts on the darkest days. When I can only see the bad, help me find the good even in the most painful moments.

7:52PM

3-25-16

Sometimes, I can't be happy for too long because I fear it might be stolen from me. Remove these negative thoughts from my mind. Bring me life.

8:17AM
3-26-16

There is just too much inside of me that I can't seem to figure out. Everything conflicts, and I keep trying to find one thing that will guide me towards the right direction. I find myself going in a circle that does not lead to anywhere. Lead me to a path that might have obstacles, but that brings me blessings.

9:23PM

3-26-16

There were times when I felt so weak that I just
couldn't get up from the ground. As humans, we
need other humans. Send me an angel.

7:13AM

3-27-16

Whenever I feel like I don't belong in the world, remind me that you have blessed me enough to open my eyes and see differently.

11:38PM

3-27-16

I want to know why we were so scared of love. I want to know why was it that we wanted it so bad yet still ran away.

10:37AM

3-28-16

Why were we so scared of our nightmares, but didn't glorify our dreams? It was almost as if we were scared to see the good in things, but we were so quick to see the bad.

2:15AM

3-29-16

I haven't been sleeping much lately. I don't know why I'm trusted with so much time. I'd like to feel a little more human.

11:14AM
3-29-16

It is 3AM and I choose to speak to you because I think that you might understand me best. I keep having these feelings come to me and it makes me think that I might possibly have a greater purpose. Help me find it. Give me what is meant to be mine and take away what is not.

3:22AM

3-30-16

There are times when my heart is so mad at my mind that it attacks it. At least, I think it does. Protect my mind from itself.

12:37PM

3-30-16

Please take away anything in my life that does not belong here. I have enough trust in you to do that.

1:06AM

3-31-16

At times, I feel as if you are unkind. I feel confined in my mind. I keep looking for emotions I don't even want to find. I am scared that I left my heart behind. Help me find it.

2:03PM

3-31-16

I keep praying to receive something that is not good
for me. Then, I get mad at you for not giving it to
me. I admit. At times, I am blind. Help me see.

11:58PM

3-31-16

You have blessed me with the gift of having a strong instinct. But, I am human and sometimes, I fail. I need you to guide me through paths that are unfamiliar.

7:57AM

4-1-16

There are consistent nights when I can't sleep. My thoughts
are dangerous and move so fast—making it impossible
for me to keep up. Provide me peace of mind.

10:13PM

4-1-16

There are times when the weight on my shoulders gets too heavy. I don't walk as if I am grateful because there are times when my thoughts consume me. This causes me to look at the world with not as much gratitude—forgetting my gifts. Please give strength to my soul so that I can carry whatever is necessary.

8:08AM

4-2-16

I have already learned that there is power in choice and
decisions because they give consequences. But, I must
not rely on only this. Help me trust destiny, too.

2:42AM

4-3-16

You have walked by my side, silently, even when
I have forgotten about you. You have never left
me alone. I just wanted to say thank you.

4:16PM

4-3-16

I have always felt like no one could understand me. I have been wondering if maybe you've noticed and that is why, lately, you have been sending me angels in human form. We'll see.

I believe in half destiny and half choice. Destiny places it there, but I know that it is up to me to grab it. The universe gravitates what is meant for me towards me, but if I am blind I'll never see it. If I don't walk towards it, I'll never reach it. If I don't reach out for it, I'll never grab it. Go after what you want. I just wanted to thank you for trusting me—a human—even when I don't always fully place my trust in you.

9:25AM
4-4-16

I feel hungry for different emotions—especially love. I often wonder why you make my heart feel so much. I feel every little feeling as if it is inside of my skin. When a feeling leaves, it takes that part of me with it, too.

11:50PM

4-4-16

Whenever I am surrounded by trust and love, I feel most whole— even when I am broken. Please never take love away from me. It is all I know. It would be enough if it were all I had.

10:12AM

4-5-16

With time, you have revealed that nothing is ever a loss. It is always just another lesson I learn. Time reveals everything that is meant for me. Every second of my life is a mystery that you know but that I am waiting to discover.

9:26PM
4-5-16

I am thankful for all the bad that occurs to me because it reveals your plan for me. It has given me strength while I have grown so that I can prepare for my future. I am learning to place my faith in you. This way, I can never truly fail even if they all think that I have.

11:28AM

4-6-16

You've given me ugly and made me dig deep. In those, which have not been the most appealing, you have shown me the greatest blessings. I'll never forget.

3:13PM

4-6-16

Sometimes I feel like I ignore your blessings because although my heart knows it, my mind is focused on something entirely different. I am sorry.

4:15AM

4-7-16

At times, I think I am deprived of love. Then, I think of all the love that lives inside of me and I question my thoughts. I know that your love for me surpasses all. And, it shows. It shows through those that you have brought in my life. It is present and it lives through them. It shows through my passions and hunger for life. You place this energy in me, daily. To me, that is enough proof that you exist.

9:42PM

4-7-16

Why did you give me a soft heart, but a strong mind?
This is a particular question that I just want to ask
you because I think about it all the time. I think those
who have this combination suffer the most because
they feel too much, but they think too much, too.

12:14PM

4-8-16

I want to know why you trust good people with pain so much as if we are the only ones who can handle it.

11:46PM

4-8-16

I have more questions for you that I feel like I will
never know the answers to. Why do you instill pain
in those we love? It is damaging to us, too.

1:19PM

4-9-16

I keep trying to look for something and find it, but I
don't know what. I don't know where to start. It is like I
am on a never-ending search. Help me find purpose.

8:36PM

4-9-16

I know that there will be obstacles along the way. Give me the strength to not stop at the distractions while I am running towards you.

3:37PM

4-10-16

I took happiness whenever it came—in parts. Some things weren't meant to be calculated. Emotions were one of them.

3:14AM

4-11-16

It is just easier to breathe. I woke up today and everything got a little better. It does get better eventually—doesn't it?

10:00PM

4-11-16

There were those rare moments when they were so happy,
they forgot how broken they were. To see them snap out of
it and remember the pain killed my heart. Heal them.

4:03AM

4-12-16

You blinded me for a reason. In the moments
of darkness, you wanted me to look within and
understand my struggle before I received blessings.

8:17AM

4-12-16

You couldn't have shown me a better way to learn how
to love selflessly. You gave me my mother. Thank you.

4:01AM

4-13-16

I have been running to you and you have been
revealing everything to me along the way. I would
have never been able to do this alone.

9:57AM

4-13-16

Please remove anything from my heart that is not
supposed to be there. I can't do it alone.

1:50PM

4-13-16

Thank you for teaching me that being alone is beautiful.
You taught me to learn every part of my heart so I
know how to use it. Before I give any part of it to
anyone, I must learn to every single thing about it.

3:33AM

4-14-16

Sometimes, you can't look for peace within because "within" is the most chaotic. In these times, I have searched for beauty in the universe. When I wanted to hide in isolation, you have saved me.

10:52PM

4-14-16

Sometimes, I wish you didn't trust me with love
so much. At times, I wish you would let me be
reckless with my heart. But, only you know.

12:05PM
4-15-16

Now that I look back and try to put all of the pieces together, I see that even in the dark there was the hidden gift of light. But, most importantly, I will never forget that in what seemed to be light, there were huge pieces of darkness.

11:51PM

4-15-16

I am praying to please remove anything and anyone
that I am not supposed to love out of my path so
I could walk the path to my soulmate faster.

4:19AM
4-16-16

Things have been coming to me when I least expect them. This makes me think that you are full of surprises. It makes me feel protected because it confirms to me that as long as I put my all into everything that I do—everything will be okay.

8:22PM

4-16-16

Even though I will never see them again, please protect them. Protect their hearts. Once I love, it can't be removed even when I am gone from their lives—permanently.

1:05AM

4-17-16

There are an endless amount of gifts in suffering. I know that sometimes they are revealed later rather than sooner. I am trying to have faith that they will be revealed on your timing.

4:01PM
4-17-16

I place my trust in you when I make any decision, no matter how small. I want you to work through me. At times, I ask for signs from you and when I do, so many are revealed. I just have to pay attention.

2:01AM

4-18-16

I could never be mad at you for putting people in my life
that needed to receive your message through me. I just ask
that you remove them from my life whenever your purpose
is complete. Some just aren't meant to be here forever.

4:00PM

4-19-16

I wanted to apologize for the times when I have almost hated you for not giving me what I thought my heart desperately wanted. I know now that you have not only saved my heart, but you have healed my mind by taking them away from me.

10:15PM
4-19-16

You have given me so much of your love, but I don't know why I just couldn't accept it. I don't know why I put up walls to block you out. I guess this was for a reason too.

8:23AM

4-20-16

I love when I wake up with a clear mind. Nothing can stop me. No one can influence me. And, not one thing can affect my decisions. Help me clear my mind and heart repeatedly—whenever I feel lost and whenever I do not know what step to take next.

12:52PM

4-21-16

I just want to know why you have given me this power
to heal but I can't self-heal. I need you to heal me, too,
since I have failed to find the power to heal myself.

9:45PM
4-21-16

I will love so much that you will become too filled. I have so much inside of me that I can't keep it in me. What makes you think that I would trust another? I think that I need to find a balance between loving the self and loving another. I always want to love so much that it leaves me. I feel like I have too much love inside of me. Did you do this on purpose?

1:31PM

4-22-16

I see it as this: children and the elderly are closer to you because they are at the beginning and end of their lives. You have shown me that they hold the most secrets. Thank you for revealing this.

11:12PM

4-22-16

Please help me learn to love time. Show me that it reveals everything. I desperately need to learn to trust it and you are the only one who can show me how. I don't know how to learn the mysteries of it alone.

11:11AM

4-23-16

Sometimes I find myself wanting to talk to you but then I don't.
Maybe it is my pride. You never talk back—you always hide.

10:10PM
4-23-16

You must love me more than I even love myself because there were times when I felt that I would have died if you weren't there to help. Thank you.

3:33AM

4-24-16

A friend came to me today and talked to me about all of her problems. She asked me for advice and I gave it to her. In those problems, I found an answer to one of mine. The world works in ways that are unexplainable to the human. I know you're looking out for me.

10:10PM

4-24-16

There is constant chaos in my thoughts. It is like a puzzle that I
can never figure out. Maybe it is because you are trying to make
me figure something out. Maybe it is my own fault because
I am constantly wanting to understand everything instead
of just being. Calm them on your time—whenever that is.

10:07PM
4-25-16

Without you, my eyes felt swollen. My mouth released words, but they all felt broken. Without you, no word was ever fulfilled even when it was spoken. My heart was numb. I was heartbroken. I was drowning in water and it felt like I was choking. How do I explain how I felt to you? I know you didn't leave, but it really felt like you were gone. God just answer! Sometimes I feel like this whole thing is a game.

Was this something that you knew all along? I hated to doubt you, but I think I know why I did. Somewhere deep inside, I knew that you are right and I was wrong. But I am only human. You should've known that this was where you belonged. I don't doubt you because maybe this was your plan. When everyone left, you showed me that on my own I could be strong. I guess I just didn't expect you to leave me feeling like this for so long. I don't want to blame you. After all this time, I know it was me who left you all along.

9:19AM
4-26-16

We're the broken. Every single thing in the world that we've come across has scarred us one way or another yet—still—they expect us to trust. We do. We're still brave. We believe in love and we try to trust. But we are also cold. So cold—that it takes something that burns us to heal us. We're contradictions.

11:07PM

4-26-16

I have watched them starve their hearts without the love that you were capable of giving them. Why do we, at times, throw away what is good for us? I couldn't do that. I could never do that. My heart needed fulfillment. It needed you. Save me.

7:11AM
4-27-16

I could never be impressed only from that which is manmade.
I knew that those material things were tangible—meaning
they would fade. My heart gravitated towards everything that
was simple and in their raw state. It gravitated towards you.

7:07PM
4-27-16

When I look at what is around me and I see what the higher
power has created—whether it be nature or humans or love,
I see a kind of beauty that shakes my entire existence. I know
what it is like to have a soul that pays attention to every little
thing that surrounds me. As a consequence, I ran far away from
anything and anyone whose eyes couldn't see the beauty in
the simple things. I ran away from anyone who couldn't make
me feel something, so strong that it moved me—to the core.

9:29AM
4-28-16

Sometimes, I want to make my heart less pure. But, then I think of you. I think of how innocent you created me. So, how could I let you down? Who would I be if I were not to use the gifts that you have blessed me with? How could I let all of that go to waste? It is possible that I have discovered my gift. We are all given many. If I have more to discover, help me search for it without stopping. I know that I have more. Help me be so in touch with myself that I can figure whatever it is you have coming for me.

11:19PM

4-28-16

I am begging for stability. Every single step feels like there is a crack on the ground and I will fall—face first. I don't know if I should stay still. Maybe that will protect me more—at least until I figure out how to put everything together. When I am unsure, protect me. I need to stabilize.

7:17AM

4-29-16

I have seen them love the idea of love—not love itself.
You can't know parts of people and call that love.
You have to know them whole. You have taught me
that love does not come in parts—it is full.

11:01PM
4-29-16

I struggle with this daily. I need to know why you have given me so much love. I don't want to question you, but I really need to know why you have trusted me with so much love. It seems like it is too strong for anyone to tolerate. Maybe it is not them. Maybe it is me. Maybe I just don't know what to do with love or how to convert it from the internal to the external. Maybe I don't know how to use this gift that you have given me properly. I just want to let you know how I feel. I want you to know that even though sometimes I doubt, I trust you. I am placing my faith in you so that you can guide me in the right direction. I will keep going and I won't give up on love. I guess I just want to tell you that I am trying. I guess that is enough.

3:37AM

4-30-16

Sometimes I wonder why you put people like us in this world. Do you want us to do something special in it? Do you want us to fix something? Do you want us to teach them something? Sometimes, everyone around me feels like they don't belong in this world. I kind of wish we could create our own. I am asking you to show us our purpose. Please.

6:07PM

4-30-16

Although I am always wondering, I am still not sure
what your plan is. I just have faith that you trust
in me to make the right decisions. But, I want you
to know that I also trust you to guide me.

9:01AM
5-1-16

My heart has been wanting to turn cold for
some time now. Help me keep it alive. There are
people out there who still need my love.

8:04PM

5-1-16

There are nights where living is hard because my
faith in everything feels shaken. The universe
can be chaotic. Help me be still.

9:45PM

5-1-16

I just want to ask you how am I supposed to trust
anything if there are times when I can't even
trust you? I always feel guilty for doubting.

10:03PM

5-1-16

I know that it seems like I am coming to you with all of these negative thoughts, but sometimes you are the only one that I can talk to. I have faith that everything will eventually turn positive if I give them to you.

10:07PM
5-1-16

Lately, I have feared letting anyone in. I have been protecting whatever is left of my insides because emotions can get messy. Help me find my center when there is turmoil.

1:05AM

5-2-16

There are days when I feel happy, but I can still feel
my sadness creeping in. Help me count my blessings
and realize that I need pain to see them.

8:15AM

5-2-16

I believe in destiny because I don't think everything can be determined by logic. But, I also believe in humans enough to know that they play a vital role.

10:33PM

5-2-16

The moments that I don't think of you are the
moments that I need you most. I am human so I
forget you. Please don't abandon me on my darkest
days. I need you to love me unconditionally.

3:13AM

5-3-16

When I distance myself from you, help me see that without you, I can't see as far. I can't see long term. I can only see what is close to me and I won't be able to figure out the consequences all on my own. I need you to guide me when I become isolated and filled with fear.

9:01AM
5-3-16

I can't be clouded. My thoughts need to be clear so that I can be aware of my surroundings. Help me figure out what is genuine faster so I can hold those things close. Please take me away from anything that is falsely coated, but that disguises itself as diamonds that are glowing. I have learned that what may be pretty to the eye is not always what it seems. Beauty lives in what is real—not in illusions.

10:17AM

5-3-16

You have gifted me with such powerful ability to love. My love is greater than anything I know. It is even greater than me. Don't let me destroy it.

5:03PM

5-3-16

I always find bits of my soul in this city. A man, who I saw playing an instrument on the street, is an example of your brilliance. He taught me a lot in a few moments. If you look close enough—with your third eye—you can find beauty in the unknown. You just can't fear it. You can be free while still being grounded. The universe moves with you. You just have to allow it.

7:09PM
5-3-16

There are mornings where I wake up and everything is a little brighter than it was the night before. You know? It is like all of the darkness becomes a little easier to get through. Everything becomes a little more peaceful. The world starts to move along with you. It will no longer feel like the world is trying to overpower you or dominate you. Even in hard moments, it will feel worth it. I have faith that those moments will come any second. I know they will.

7:29PM
5-3-16

I look at the words that leave their mouths and I become scared for them. I know that they are lost in confusion. Not everything is temporary. Real love is immortal. It doesn't end—even with death. Permanence lives in love.

8:14PM

5-3-16

Gravitate me towards the good, which will include eliminating all of what I hold close that is disguised as love. Even if it will hurt me, I know that it will be for my greater good. Only you know.

3:33AM

5-4-16

I can see my future in his eyes—just like he can see
passed my lies—like how strongly I love beyond
the cold disguise. Have you placed him here?

11:13AM

5-4-16

I have learned that to be able to love is a blessing and any blockage will hinder my greatest power. Allow me to trust in it enough so that I remain open to any blessing coming my way.

11:56PM

5-4-16

Maybe I need to stop trying to figure everything out. Maybe I don't hold all the answers. I mean that is why you are here, right?

1:07AM
5-5-16

I am praying for one sign. One sign that everything will be okay. I am looking for something that will help me look forward to another day. We can't communicate directly, but I just want you to show me that you hear me. I want to know that you feel me. I just want something. Anything. Maybe the proof is in me breathing. Maybe the proof is in me just me existing. Maybe. Just don't think that I don't notice. I do. I notice everything.

1:29AM
5-5-16

Being alive is something that we all take for granted at one point or another. We hold so much power inside of us that we hold the ability to make great changes in the world. It all starts with the self. I have found that every single thing that we do affects something or someone. We are all important even though the world is so big. Help me make the change that is needed. Help me help someone.

2:07AM
5-5-16

I trust you. I am guessing that is a powerful thing—you know? To trust something that no one has proven to exist—at least that is what they say. But, regardless, you are greater than proof. Or maybe they think that they don't have proof because they search for something that can be seen instead of just feeling what the eyes cannot see. Maybe the proof that you exist is inside of us—not outside of us. Maybe we should reverse our searching.

3:01AM

5-5-16

Sometimes I feel so close to everything as if I can almost reach
it, but then it escapes my hands. It escapes me completely
and this is the exact moment that I become stuck. I don't
know if it is because I don't try hard enough or if it is because
it just isn't meant for me—whatever that thing may be. I
know that most things are in your power but I know you
also give me power. I wish I could know why. I wish you
could speak to me in a way I can understand—just once.

4:38AM

5-5-16

I guess that I have noticed that we are afraid to love because of the consequences. Every single time we have tried to love, the hurt has always been more unbearable. Or—has it? Because if that is really the case, we wouldn't need love to heal us. It is ironic, right? Love heals and love hurts us. My heart told me to let you know this. I don't know why. Maybe I need love tonight and my hurt is not letting me receive it.

5:01AM

5-5-16

It is hard to remain peaceful when there is a war going on in my head. It is almost as if I am fighting for peace. Isn't that ironic? Take the negative thoughts away from our minds and turn them into positive fuel.

5:55AM
5-5-16

There are times when I feel so strong, but there are other times when I feel terribly weak. The instability of emotions can be draining—to the point where the highs and the lows are too much to bear. But, then I think of the way that I trust in you.

I think of all of the ways that you would want me to learn from these experiences and use them towards something else. I know that there is beauty in everything—somewhere. I believe this—even if you have to dig deep because you can't see it on the surface. Everything you have touched holds blessings.

We just have to find them. I promise to make it a goal to find all of the blessings that I can in this lifetime. I have learned that I can't do that if I doubt in my power.

1:09PM
5-5-16

My mind can be poisonous. Some of my thoughts have the ability to hurt me. I know that there is pain and suffering in the world, but help my mind not constantly notice the negative. In what may seem terrible, live hidden meanings.

2:01PM

5-5-16

I woke up thankful today. I woke up remembering all of the little things that I am happy for. But, although I am still thankful, as the day progresses and it gets closer to the night, I always seem to get a little anxious. I forget what I am thankful for—or maybe I don't forget, but everything just starts to get a little overwhelming. The night comes near and it is as if all of these negative thoughts enter my mind. Help me remain positive.

3:03PM

5-5-16

Sometimes, I doubt love. I fear that it is an illusion that humans create and that it is something that just takes place in our mind. It is hard to believe because it is not tangible. But, then I think about this again. Love can be tangible. So, it isn't true because there are certain forms of love that can be seen and felt. There is proof of love in the humans who hold parts of my heart. I guess I was writing you this to speak to myself after all. It was never to question you.

4:45PM

5-5-16

The power lies in our hearts and in our minds. Anything
we think and feel—we can manifest. The love that
we want—we can create from within us. The way our
souls see the world is shaped within us. And, we? Well,
we hold that power. Never take that for granted.

5:09PM
5-5-16

Whenever I feel most disconnected with the world, there are two things I want to do. I want to either isolate myself and find myself in my own world or I need to be around people so that I can learn parts about myself in them. Help me learn the times that give me the best peace of mind. However, if you find me choosing isolation too often, help me choose the latter.

5:19PM
5-5-16

There are times when I fear that my focus is on the wrong things. I fear that I don't pay attention. I know that if I don't pay attention, my calling will not be visible. I won't see what is meant for me and I might miss it. I need to be aware of not only my surroundings, but I need to be aligned with my insides. I need to not only listen to my mind, but my heart.

6:07AM
5-6-16

Maybe we all think that we can't see the most important
things. Maybe we can see love. Maybe we can see sadness.
Maybe we can see all of these emotions. We just have
to try to see what is unseen. We have to believe—that
is something no one can give us. That is something we
have to give ourselves. We have to believe in ourselves, in
our souls, and in who we are. We have to believe in the
universe. We have to believe that it all aligns, eventually.

7:01PM

5-6-16

I could sit here wondering what will happen or I
could take this next breath and live. I could wish for
something, but then my blessings might be overlooked.
The universe is not my enemy. It is my friend. I know
that whatever may come is written for me. I just have to
trust in that. Yeah, I guess I have to just trust in that.

9:09PM
5-6-16

Maybe I should stop searching for all of these answers. Maybe sometimes, I just need to feel. Maybe if something is not given to me, freely, then it wasn't meant to be given to me at all. I am constantly stuck between free will and fate. If the human remains idle, will one get what is meant to come even if one does not work towards what one wants? Will it come regardless? I have too much faith in the human to believe that the human does not play a part.

10:54PM
5-6-16

Sometimes, I look at everything that has happened in the past and everything kind of pieces together. Every single time that I thought everything was about to crash, I was given better. There were times when I have suffered so tremendously that the thought still pains me to this day. But, it has still built me up to who I am and I am thankful for it all. I hope that I am reminded that my struggles are small bumps for what is to come tomorrow. There are many more blessings. Always.

7:09AM
5-7-16

Going through certain things and being brought up in a certain environment taught me one thing: to adapt to anything. I think that being able to adapt without changing who you are at your core is really important. We all need to learn how to adapt to any given situation. Let no surprise affect you that tremendously that you are not able to handle it or deal with it. I couldn't have done it without your guidance.

8:05PM
5-7-16

There is a rush of fear that enters my body that sometimes puts me in a paralytic state. It is as if I don't know what will happen next. But then I remember that there is nothing that you would put me through if I wouldn't be able to deal with it. I am able to and I must repeat this to myself. Whatever it is I think, I know that I can do. Whatever it is that is given to me, I know can be done.

9:31PM

5-7-16

You have brought me things that I did not know I needed at the times when I least expected them or at times when I didn't even want them. I doubted you, but now I know that if those things did not happen, I would not be here right now. I am trying to accept everything with open arms and an open heart.

11:03PM

5-7-16

Life can be a mystery—or do we just tell ourselves that so that we can become distracted? Maybe we already know what we want and we are just scared to go after it. Is all we do irrelevant when it comes to destiny or do we have a say in what happens? I refuse to believe that wishing without doing causes certain things to come to life.

11:33PM

5-7-16

The closer I get to you, the more I realize that I shouldn't really regret anything as long as I know that all I have done was done with the best intentions at heart. Of course I know that I have made mistakes because I am human and I am heavily flawed. You have shown me that the more I stay alert in my every action while trusting the universe to give me the signs, the more I find where I am supposed to be in life and what I should do next.

11:53PM

5-7-16

I started living when I realized that I couldn't escape from myself. I was here in the world and I realized that I had to make the best out of it. No one had more power over my life, except for me...and you. I know that you would always want what is best for me even though this world, at times, could be damaging. You've always been there to help me save myself.

11:58PM

5-7-16

Every person I come across has a message for me. I know it. I only fear that some come with a message that will harm me even though I know that every single person teaches me something regardless. Help me remain open and not close myself off from everyone because of this irrational fear that I have. Help me follow my heart and not only rely on my mind.

3:00AM
5-8-16

I know that there is pain and that there is struggle. At times, I feel it more than ever, but in order to bloom and in order to grow, I know that I have to go through all of this. Some people have it harder than others. Life isn't easy, but it is worth it. We are seeds. Some are lucky enough to get sunlight right away— they bloom without much struggle. But others—you see—other seeds stay in the dark for too long and the sun doesn't always shine on them. They get sunlight very late in life. But you see—those flowers are the most beautiful because they bloom even when everyone was expecting them to die.

10:01AM

5-8-16

I constantly think about the future and where I will be a few years from now. The only answer that I can think of— if I am true to myself—is that I see myself at peace. The riches and the fame are all irrelevant. I just want peace and I want to learn how to provide it to as many humans as possible. Peace of mind goes a long way. Maybe I won't reach complete happiness or love, but I will reach stages of it.

10:51PM

5-8-16

Everything was slowly starting to align and that in itself
was enough to keep going even through all of the fear and
even through all that has ever been broken. It was enough
to keep searching for peace, for happiness, and for love.
Each smile meant something. It meant hope. All of these
three things lie within each of us, but it is up to us to not
block them out. It is up to us to embrace them. And I
promise—more than ever—to let what is meant enter me.

11:16PM

5-8-16

I could never settle. I don't have the heart to do that. Protect my thoughts from even attempting to take that route. That is a dangerous mediocre life that my heart has no desire to take part in.

11:31PM

5-8-16

There are plenty of times when I am unsure of what will
happen, like tonight, but I think that is where my part
comes in. I can't rely on you for everything. I have to take
chances even though I am not sure that I will get what I
want. As long as I want something and it is aligned with my
mind and my heart, it is worth a try. It is up to you whether
you decide to give it to me or not. All in your hands.

1:01AM

5-9-16

When you ask God to show you signs, he does. You just
have to pay attention to everything—as if everything
holds something that is potentially yours and you need.

3:41PM

5-9-16

Sometimes it pains me to think of what I feel whenever I close my eyes. So, there are times when I don't want to sleep. I can't sleep. They say that sleep distracts you. They say that it makes you escape it all. But, what do I do when I can't escape it? What do I do when I go to bed and I get the same result when I wake up? In my sleep, I am not in control. It is ironic because when I'm awake, I'm not either. But, when I am awake—at least I can try. Or maybe I can't and I create an illusion. Maybe it is all destiny and I fool myself thinking that I can control it when it escapes from my hands every time I try to reach for it. And I guess that is what paralyzes me the most. I don't want to move because I know the outcome every single time. So, I just stay still in hopes that you will fix it. I doubt you at times because we fight for what is best for me every second of the day... but I still talk to you. So what does that say about me? That I only believe in existence when the result is in my favor? I'm just telling you my thoughts. I know they are all over the place.

7:19PM
5-9-16

I never thought that I would get to where I am. I never thought that I would get through everything, but I didn't give up. I took a risk to get through the darkness in order to search for light. To be honest, I still can't hold on to happiness too tight because I know that there are times when it will escape me. But, the beauty is that I have learned a lesson. I have learned to enjoy it while I can.

8:15PM

5-9-16

I guess I am just terrified. I have seen good people not appreciated and I have seen them become damaged. I have seen innocence stolen. I have seen the world hurt them over and over again. I have seen true and real love, all forms, not just the romantic kind—killed: sometimes intentionally and sometimes unintentionally. I have seen loyalty become weak. I have seen it all disappear in the blink of an eye. I have seen those most in touch with the universe become shattered along with it. I have seen those who deserved everything get nothing. Despite all of this, I see beauty in its highest form. I have seen them keep going even though they were hurting. The strength I have seen in them has been inspirational. I have seen them keep living—with hope. I am asking you something, just one thing. Please, don't kill their last hope. Give them love.

9:50PM

5-9-16

We are only here for a certain amount of time. Why do some of us, at times, including myself, forget that? We hurt ourselves and we hurt others. We don't take care of ourselves fully—so how can we take care of the world? We are trying, but we are only human. I am only human. How do we get to be like you? How do we get to hold so much power, but still be gentle and forgiving? How do we remain positive and see the beauty in everything? How?

You know how some people think of the future and fear fills them up because they don't know what is coming? They don't know where they will be. They don't know if their next breath is certain—let alone anything else. Uncertainty fills them. But you know, with me—it is something a little stronger. It is the present that I fear. It is supposed to be certain, right? I am supposed to be certain that I am alive. I am here. But, that is my problem. I am not certain about my present. It is uncertain for me. It is unstable. I don't know what to make out of present moments because I am unsure about them. I know nothing about them. You can never be too certain. That is all I wanted to tell you for now.

10:09PM
5-10-16

This world holds so much greatness—some that is hidden and some that is seen. You have created a heart like mine that sees beauty in everything. If I know something out there holds pain, it is hard for me to maintain happiness as a constant. I feel for everything in the world and the way it moves, not just for myself. I wouldn't be able to feel just for myself.

10:26AM

5-11-16

Love spilled out of the cracked wounds of my heart. Although I wanted to remain closed—so desperately— there was no way I could hold it in any longer. This was no way to live. They could hear my insides screaming. I will be open. I need to be open.

11:11PM

5-11-16

Don't let me rush, but whenever it is that my heart notices something good, don't let me fear commitment either. I think that this world is so fast paced and we see everything as coming and going that we constantly search for what is better, ignoring what we have. I think that is our biggest mistake. Don't let me settle, but help me recognize when a soul is similar to mine. Using souls in any way is something that shouldn't be done. They should be kept safe. So help me do that. I need you.

9:34AM
5-12-16

There is something that I've seen. I have seen people hurt not only others, but themselves. I've seen them suffer terribly, so much that it has broken their own hands holding on to pride so tightly. Why do this to ourselves and those we love? Is it because we are flawed humans? Maybe so, but I think we have too much heart to allow something so weak to get in the way. We are poisoning ourselves at the expense of love. When I think of being prideful, don't let me follow that path.

11:59PM
5-12-16

It is like chemicals and although I can't explain it, I know
what it is well. My soul knows what it is well. It is like
everything that I have inside of me is organizing itself so
that it aligns perfectly with what was meant for me. It is
as if my heart, soul, and mind are not one yet, but they
are beginning to understand each other—so well that I
am finally starting to understand who I am. I couldn't
describe how filled with peace I am. I guess I am healing.

3:03AM

5-13-16

When I speak, allow me to be mindful of the words that leave my mouth. I've heard too many broken promises spoken—so many, that words have weakened. The power of words are great and it is a terrible thing when someone hears something and cannot take it for its meaning, but always searches for an ulterior motive behind it. Help my words be as genuine and honest as possible to alleviate this problem for others.

6:01PM

5-13-16

There is so much to see that is hidden even though it is right in front of us. Whenever I am blind, open my eyes. I like to find meaning in everything because I know everything has meaning behind it. Nothing just is without explanation. Everything has a story.

9:05PM
5-13-16

There are times, like right now, when I can't point out to what it is wrong, but I know I hold heavy burdens within me. Help my mind remain calm while my insides fight wars that my brain might never understand. My heart feels too much and, at times, I don't even think my mind can understand. Maybe it isn't meant to. Maybe this is meant for a reason. I can be sensitive, but only because I am fighting my hardest to not become desensitized. Thank you for listening, again. You always do.

9:51PM

5-13-16

My mind is telling me that I am numb, but I feel all of these emotions inside of me. I am beginning to wonder how it is possible to seem like I feel nothing to the world when my mind and heart feel more than ever. I don't know the answer to that, but I do hope you look over those dealing with silent battles. Although the others may not hear our silent cries, I know you hear them the loudest.

1:03AM

5-14-16

When it feels like there is a fire burning deep down inside of me and it doesn't allow me to turn any energy that I may have into a positive force, please eliminate it from my body. Allow no source that does not derive from peace make its home here. I don't want to disrupt the good mental state in which I may be at. And when anger arrives, and I am sure it will because I am human, allow it to not destroy the good in me—no matter what situation may come my way.

10:18PM

5-14-16

Sometimes there is this feeling inside of me that starves for certain things: like peace of mind and love. During these times, I am most vulnerable and strong—at the same exact time because I will do whatever it takes to fulfill my passion and grab whatever it is that I feel is missing from me, but belongs to me. Make sure I have enough power over myself to not abandon what I need in order to get what I want.

9:01AM
5-15-16

I crave human emotion from empty souls. There is
something about people coming to life and living when
all hope was lost. This is the beauty of the broken and
waking them up to see beauty in everything that is around
them is a gift that not many are able to witness.

9:03PM
5-15-16

I am at a place and I feel still. I don't know if that is a good or a bad thing, but I am just unsure what exactly will happen next. I am not sure if good or bad things will come. All I know is that I am ready for you to take me to whatever path you want—not what I want. I am ready for whatever comes my way, but I also know that I can't and won't be able to just rely on you. I need to rely on myself. I need whatever I think to manifest. Only I can create it. You have given me a gift and I know that I need to use it. I can't let it go to waste and just blame you for things not happening. Thank you.

3:00AM

5-16-16

They might call us different, but really, this is only truth to
blind eyes. We are all human, and had they looked closer,
they would see our souls are connected and see the truth
passed society's invisible lines. You created us all equal.
Most fail to see that this will be humanity's demise.

10:00AM
5-16-16

I came by the water today and I just want to thank you for my existence. The world is good, but there is also a lot of bad in it. We have choice over not everything, but some things. And today, I choose to just be thankful for my existence. It gets really hard sometimes but I believe in you fully. If I didn't have a purpose, I wouldn't be here. And I'm here for something even though I haven't figured everything out yet. Maybe I'm not meant to figure everything out. Maybe I need to stop searching for answers right away. Maybe time will reveal it all. Sometimes I just get tired of waiting. You know best though, God. I am sure of it. Thanks for always listening even when others might have not.

2:01AM

5-17-16

I have learned that they will tell you that you feel too much—
you know, that you shouldn't do every little thing with
your whole heart. They will try to tell you that you aren't
realistic in hopes that you will become desensitized, like
them. They fail to see that we are so in touch with ourselves
that we become a part of the universe. We not only get
happiness from everything, but we bleed with everything
too. They fail to realize that our hearts might belong with
the universe and are strong like it, too. Help me hold on to
who I am. I don't want to become desensitized. I refuse.

I am writing to you, but I don't want to bother you. My conversations with you never stop. I always have something to say to you. I know that you are supposed to know everything, but at this moment I am unsure if you do. If you really knew everything, I just want to know why are you letting me go through this? Sorry. Forget it. I don't want to question you. That is never my intention. I just want to talk and I don't know if you know how I feel at this moment. And if anyone were to know, I want it to be you. I feel still. I feel like I can't move and like I'm stuck in one place. I think about all of these small things because I am terribly indecisive. I think about the smallest things and make them huge. I guess you do know what you are doing. You hold power, but remember, that I don't forget that you gave me power too. And I'm trying. I really am. I guess I have to figure it out. Just guide me.

11:00PM

5-17-16

I have noticed that the world has given me what I have given it and when it hasn't, I noticed that, in itself, was a gift too.

11:57PM

5-17-16

Sometimes they may try and sometimes they may put in no effort, but remind me that the power you have placed within me is never to go unused. If it does, I have wasted my own power and what a tragedy that would be.

8:19AM
5-18-16

Finality. I often wonder what that means. Does it mean that there is nothing coming after it or does it mean that one chapter is closed and we are blindly moving on to the next, waiting for a blessing or a lesson? For me, it means that I might not know what comes next, but I am trying to live every second as if it is a gift given to me. Sometimes, I want you to know that it is impossible to do that. Not because I don't value what you have given me. Not because I am taking your love for granted. But, because hope seems to eliminate from my body and I do not forget its definition because although my heart believes, my mind has trouble with it. Help me remember that whenever something is in its final stages, it is meant to come to an end. I hope to remember to hold close every moment just in case I will be too hopeless when it leaves my hands. And at the moment it leaves my hands, help me remember that it was meant to. Whatever is final will be mine once again if it is in your plan.

11:07PM

5-18-16

When it has left me, whatever it may be, do not let me be devastated—even when it may hurt so bad that it may feel like it is cutting me into little pieces. Let me see whatever it may be as a blessing because it is you trying to show me something. Let me accept whatever pain it may be as long as I know that it will eventually be alleviated. There are times when I feel like I try to make myself believe these lies. But, then I remember that they are not lies because whenever times passes, you show me different. Always. I may be a lost soul, but even then, I have faith that you know the timing in which I will be found.

1:02PM
5-19-16

I have noticed that some would rather be comforted and silenced by lies as long as they avoid the truth. May I accept whatever change comes my way as long as I keep who I am at my core. As long as I remain a flawed human who has so much faith in you that I cannot be moved to anything that might hurt my soul. Help my soul remain pure even when they are begging to taint it.

11:41PM

5-19-16

"Life is short." Yeah, I have heard that so many times. But, that only holds true if you don't use every second that was given to you. I've been there before. I remember praying and asking you why was I placed in certain positions. I was trying to figure out why I felt a certain why. I was trying to understand everything that was happening to me. I was trying to put all of the pieces together. But, I realized, that doing exactly this meant that I wasn't living. I was breathing, but I wasn't living. And, believe me when I tell you that there is a difference. I want to thank you for opening my eyes and allowing me to see everything so different at such a young age. I have learned to use pain as a gift.

4:09PM
5-20-16

I call it pressure. Sometimes it gets too much and it feels like I don't have it in me to fight, but at other times it feels like I have all the weight of the world on my shoulders for a reason. I do this not only for myself, but I do this for them. I do it for those who still need something to inspire them. It is energy and we all give it to each other. We have the power to choose whether the pressure will defeat us or push us to keep going. I just feel like sometimes it consumes me. And, I often wonder at what point does it become a moving force or a crippling force to my humanity. Help me find balance.

11:51PM

5-20-16

They tell me that I have trouble moving forward because I keep thinking about the past. I think they're wrong. I think they all paint that as a bad thing, but I just don't see it as that. The past is a part of you and in order to fully accept myself, I feel like I have to come to peace with everything and try to understand everything. I know that not everything is meant to be understood, but I don't want to avoid things and leave certain wounds unhealed. I want to go back and heal them to the best of my ability so that I can know where I came from, but not let it dictate where I am going. I feel like they want you to become numb to who you were, but I wouldn't be okay with being who I am if I didn't know where I came from. I feel like it would all be an illusion. So, I want you to know that I have been looking at my past lately, but instead of focusing on the "what ifs," I have been seeing the bigger picture. I have been seeing that it all connects, in one way or another. Help me know myself well while still being able to move forward.

10:01AM
5-21-16

It is difficult to maintain a pure soul in a world where materials hold such high value. We are taught to hold materialistic things close to us since we were young. We are rewarded with gifts as presents or we are rewarded with things if we do a good deed or we are given presents on holidays. All of that is beautiful, but I think that it has conditioned us to not feel to our full potential. I think that it has forced us to forget that what is free is sometimes too beautiful of a gift. Sometimes, we forget that what is unseen and what is felt are gifts in themselves. We just have to find them—somewhere inside of us. Help me find all that lives inside of me before looking for what is outside.

Tonight, I don't just want to talk to you, but I want to ask you a question. How do I let love leave me, but still keep it? I guess I just want to know if it is possible to not be so cold and fear love leaving me. I know my strength and I know the way I love, but I don't know if someone else will take care of it in the same way that I do. I know that it is a risk that is worth taking, but I don't want to give my love to someone who isn't meant for me. Help me figure this out, somehow.

1:57AM

5-22-16

Waiting doesn't seem so bad when you have hope that something good will come. But, how about those times when I feel unsure? How about those times when we don't have hope at all? What do we do then? I believe that only you know the answer, so I will stop trying to figure it out. I have no choice, but to let it be. Only you know what is best for me.

3:00AM

5-22-16

I wanted to share this with you. Lately, I have been finding more beauty in that which I have never seemed to notice before. Maybe I am growing, and with growth comes better understanding. Sometimes, you see beauty in different ways. Chemistry, connection, and love…yeah, love. Anything that knows love and holds it within them is too beautiful to put into words. Thank you for bringing them along my path.

3:03AM

5-23-16

Not everything exists. Sometimes, you have to dig deep into yourself to create you. I have learned that I have seeds growing within me, but it is up to my mind, my heart, and every other part of me to allow its roots to grow. And, when it grows, they need to allow it to flow outside of me. I have learned that this does not mean that my roots will die, if I take care of them. It just means that I have control over what is inside of me and that I will allow it to leave me just so I can create something that I didn't think was possible to have exited before. I hold that power. I can create what I believe in with my whole being. And when they don't believe that love exists, I will prove to them otherwise—through your power.

3:57AM

5-23-16

May I never become angered or confused whenever I feel like I am giving too much of myself to anyone. May I remember that sometimes people are placed on this earth to give more than they are given because God's message needs to be worked through them. Some feel a greater responsibility to be sensitive to some than others. I am okay with being used to my greatest ability as long as it will not cause me great harm in the future.

5:57AM
5-23-16

There were so many times where I thought that these little details were pointless, but as time passed I saw that they were all parts of a bigger meaning. The message is sometimes hidden, but it will reveal itself with time. You just have to keep going. I just have to learn to trust more. I need to learn to just be more. Being in itself deals with great courage.

6:03AM

5-23-16

I would give up everything I have for a love that is real—
selflessly—but as I have moved along with time, I have become
smart enough to know that love would never do that. It
doesn't take. It gives—planting seeds, not cutting the roots.

We all have different beliefs, and I respect them all. But, for me, God exists— and not just outside of us. I wouldn't have been able to have found him if I didn't look within me and find myself, first. When I found myself, I started to trust him more and I learned that he was within me even when I was lost.

And when you are lost, look to the sky…
When no one else is there, have faith that your tears, He will dry…
When you are fallen, He will fix your wings, just so you can fly…
When it feels like all is broken, I hope you know that this too shall pass and you will get by…
All of my guidance comes from The Most High…
When they ask me why…
I will say that when they all left, He stayed by my side…
He said hello after they all said goodbye.

Love,
Magi

P.S. Thank you for loving me unconditionally.

3